Thou[illegible] waking

Thoughts on Waking

Poems

Rachel Ferguson

r f l press

First published in 2023 by RFT Press
1-7-6 Sugamo
Toshima-ku
Tokyo
170-0002 www.rachelferguson.net

Cover artwork by Annie Kurkdjian

Typesetting and design by Abrar Ahmed

ISBN - 978-1-3999-5792-2

For Mum.
You always said, "One day, you'll understand."
I think I do.

Table of Contents

Thoughts on Waking

For Norman MacCaig

The pilgrims with chaotic eyes
wept, wailing and kissing the walls
of the Orthodox church
where frescoes and gold icons
promised the poor and infirm
deliverance from their suffering
though at what price
was unclear.

After the third church in the tour,
choked by ennui as each site
blended to one crumbling
edifice, I stopped talking
to the hostel boy with whom
I'd spent the night out of boredom.
Boredom and
loneliness.

Downcast by my indifference,
I sat, for the last few stops,
in the car with the driver,
smoking his cigarettes,
wondering why they were crying,
and why they thought doing it
near all those faded blues and gold
would finally
make God care.

I was understanding, thighs stuck
to the blistering vinyl seat
that nothing sacred
requires a translator
or a guide working for tips:
the loyal moon is holy,
three trillion blessed rocks and trees,
my partially
tarnished heart.

Shared Sleep

"Love does not make itself known through the desire for copulation... but in the desire for shared sleep." Milan Kundera, The Unbearable Lightness of Being.

You say you cannot sleep when we're too close
or face to face;
always turn away, not through choice
but necessity;
just can't settle down when your skin
is touching skin.
It's you.
It's not me.
I must not take it personally.

After making love, you kiss me once,
squeeze me —
a firm full stop.
Then,
almost immediately,
          roll , roll, away
                    (an arm's length away but it feels so
                                        far away)
and drift off
easily.

Unknown to you, love,
then comes the disloyalty:
your body betrays you
with brazen discourtesy.

A leg snakes back.
Toes outstretched,
your foot finds my foot
and they dance
a slow serpentine dance
before our ankles hook.
Sunflower to the sun you turn,
take hold of my thigh.
I hold
my breath...
            and watch until...
                        your brow smooths...
                                    you sigh ....

and I get what I've been waiting for:
your thinking self erased,
in one clean sweep you bind me,
wrap your arm around my waist,
your hands cradle curves,
my hip welds to your chest and
when each limb is interlaced,
your head lays on my breast.

Here you sleep.
Here you dream.
Here you are confessed.

BTW

My love is not a ransom note.
I won't post you a severed toe
if you don't love me back.

I may not even tell you
since I don't need permission
and, frankly, it's none of your business.

But if, one day,
it does slip from my lips
don't respond; it's not a question,
just information plain as
what I had for tea last night.

You wouldn't say thank you
to that, would you?
Or pretend you had spaghetti too
just to be polite?

Bulletproof

Concealed beneath your tailored suit
your armour stays true,
still unseen as we undress.

I never could have guessed
you needed cladding to protect you

but now see I was disarmed,
by sorrow as well as charm.
How can you breathe?

Have you everything you need
to live the life you want unharmed?

Have you ever knelt and cried
your lungs out an ocean wide
just to feel fresh air rush in?

Can love live in your skin
when your heart's been fortified?

Sakura

Ash-like stour corrupts the view from the lounge
but there's no sign of fire on the grounds.
A small wedding party takes photographs
on a lacquered bridge, red as the bride's lips,
while pallid blossoms obfuscate the air,
surging and waning, settling
on her silk hood like snow on untouched snow,
dusting the shoulder of the groom's kimono.

From quivering branches,
petals are torn by mellow gusts
soft as a thing newborn.
Heard only by bombilating bees,
they alight on the glistening pond beneath
trapped in the surface, as if in honey,
forming a blanket neither dry nor warm,
while the freshly wed memorialise
the spot we stood one evening watching fireflies.

The petals will vanish in a few days,
photos will fade but the trees always
bloom again. "Just wait! You must be patient!"
I want to shout to the bride, "Don't fret!
It's not all hearts and butterflies but love
is not like that — at least there is no fire!"
But cliches lack power for hot-blooded souls
who don't care for flowers. Give us infernos.

Loss of a Half-Formed Thing

false start
jumped the gun
little loaf
underdone

mindless pipe dream
stunted seed
dumb idea
ill-conceived

undeveloped
photo spool
tasteless teaser
april fool

careless joy
boastful lie
silly unsung
lullaby

partial poem
pencil sketch
briefly human
little wretch

faulty pea-brain
feeble heart
benign growth
scrape it out

Un-announce it
toss out names
stomach pity
bury shame

lipstick lips
put on shoes
black mascara
waterproof

Fall

Blossoms have long withered in the orchard.
Nature sheds her womb's rich pulp,
empties her lungs, sets up to rest.
Boughs that bore the burden of the crop
release their grip, letting their charges fall
unharvested. Thudding down, split and bruised,
they moulder in the sodden mulch
like babies in afterbirth: a chaos
of wasted potential blistering
the soil, chances condemned to
to rot beneath an atrophying sun.
All that I desire is to catch one.

Apple

Let me lay my thoughts on the coolness of you.
My tears slide off your skin
like raindrops on a window.
You protect yourself well.

Let me rest my shattered brain on your
wholeness,
the reassuring density,
the fidelity of your
appleness,
green and unbruised,
crisp as youth,
sure as sense,
so robustly you.

Let me stop awhile in your quietness
to contemplate
your unimpeachable core,
the poise of tight, modest flesh
conceals reservoirs,
that exquisite crush
of sour and sweet.

The First Leg

Summer's a barrel of maggots.
My teeth clench against the heave
in viscid heat.

Butterflies hatch in autumn.
Wing-beats hushed as lashes
pulse silvering skin
on amber-lit eves.

A cairn is raised in winter:
claggy enclave confining
savage contortions
o writhing survivor,
my fattening beast.

Clock wound to spring,
sluggish limbs, slick as tar,
unfurl like silk
with untaught ease,
head south to see
labour complete

but once emerged,
defenceless fool,
you'll wish only
to retreat
to retreat
to retreat.

Natural?

not the way you were conceived
with a shot of HCG
a scheduled lunchtime fuck
and messy pessaries,

not the needles and X-rays
when my waters broke,
or your stuttering heart
tracked with electrodes,

not the pethidine that scrambled me
when I wouldn't open
the way I had been hoping
after all that hypnobirthing,

not the spinal tap
I begged for fifteen hours in,
flinging my birth plan
in the sterile hazard bin,

not the soft electro beats
that carried me through
silvery stretches
of the loneliest night,

not how they slit me wide
and yanked you out with
giant salad tongs,
barely missing your eye,

not how alien you were,
like a stranger to me,
nothing in your face
I even faintly recognised,

not the lightening in my veins
like a tingling heart attack
and the love flooding my blood
that first time you latched,

not taking you home
in a taxi next day,
like pilots without permits,
thieves in a getaway.

Every moment since
has defied the rational:
Motherhood is nothing
if not supernatural.

Four Days Old

A swimmer crossing the channel, goose
fat-smeared flesh, purplish underneath.
Pickled grub, I drink you in,
my tequila worm.

Eyes like soft fruit, lids sliced
neat as blades of grass, papaya-seed
pupils dart this way and that.
You're right not to trust me.

Today, I took you home, cut your nails and
snipped off the tips of your matchstick fingers.
Blood seeped like watercolour.
My first mistake.

Tokyo Morning

I'm writing this between mouthfuls
of the breakfast I prepared
but didn't get to eat
before the school run.

The workday, well underway,
greets me through the screen door:
trains that scream by night
zoom coolly to a stop behind a
winsome station jingle.
Cars hum politely.
Kindergarten voices and
delivery truck doors are an
urban calypso graced by birdsong.

It's fruit if you're wondering:
melon, mango, blueberries and
yoghurt with a puddle of sakura honey
bought from a Hayama roadside last week.
Coffee in my favourite cup,
microwaved again.

The collage of litter on the living room floor:
fairy wings, picture books,
abandoned pyjamas,
a sandwich wedged in the couch cushions
are masterful brushstrokes
abstract accents on the
canvas of the day.

Here is my life:
the mess, the trains,
stale coffee,
this pen.

The Gift

En route to my house for a small party,
my friend met my son on the street with his gran,
carrying the cake they had made for my birthday
and he (he was three) told my friend about me,
my birthday, the cake: "She's so lovely," he said.

Every day since, I find pause in the rush
to untie the ribbons of this souvenir,
still fresh as the day it was carried to me,
letting the sweet morsel melt into my tongue,
infusing my bloodstream with love.

Education

Today, six-year-old Grace
learnt to stand atop a horse
so that after a morning
of unbridled riding
wherever her heart needs to go,
she can jump up and pluck
the best apples from their bough,
one for her and one for the horse.

You Can't Fit a Square Peg in a Round Hole

Chaser of Butterflies
Dismantler of Gadgets
Pusher of Buttons
Giver of Rocks
Bestower of Kisses
Greeter of Strangers
Discarder of Clothes
Rain Dancer

I will stand guard.
I will stand guard.

I wish we were all more like you

On Reading David Graham's "Listening for Your Name"

You thrust yourself upon me.
I lay down my book.

(I've been teaching you how to read
my mind this Christmas:
"Ok, it's a fruit," I say,
"Pineapple?" your voice rings
sweet with hope.
"How'd you do that!" I cry, and then,
"Alright, a number."
Your eyes close, you scrunch your nose,
"Seven-twenty hundred?"
"Genius!" I declare and
watch you swell with pride.)

I lay down my book
take up your face,
see you for the first time.
How holy! How good!
Your smile strikes my chest.
"Are you crying, Mum?"
You root for the root

of the feeling you feel.
"No, baby. A poem I just read
got stuck, right in here."
You roll your little self over my knees,
the silk of your hair slipping
through my hands,
and ask to play the game again.
"Tell me what I'm thinking," I say and
send it through my eyes.
"You love me."
You're sure this time
and, this time,
you're right.

Girls Trip

An hour from the city,
time-worn seaside town,
convenience store dinner
in our dressing gowns,
Fast and Furious 9
in the hotel lounge.
I'd watch the whole franchise
with you by my side.

Laying all morning
curled up like yin and yang
nose nudging your cheek
breast under your hand
watching cartoons on YouTube
lazing without plans.
My favourite place with you
is anywhere, nothing to do.

Then you lift my shirt,
grab your pad and pen.
I won't hide myself from you,
not now at just-turned seven
or even when you're seventy
(God, let me live till then,
to feel the wrinkles on your hands
sitting together without plans).

The Ripe Fruit Must Be Eaten

A minute is a season.
Yesterday's child is gone.
The ripe fruit must be eaten.

In presence, flavours deepen:
each moment halcyon.
A minute is a season.

The sentimental cheapens
the beauty of the dawn.
The ripe fruit must be eaten.

We're now and now in Eden.
The future is a con.
A minute is a season

when universes sweeten.
The past is but a yawn.
The ripe fruit must be eaten.

In desire, we weaken,
become the ego's pawn.
A minute is a season.
The ripe fruit must be eaten.

Mother Tongue

I was five years old
when you and your friend
had me speak in tongues.

I'd just come in to
get some water when
you called me over.

Your friend prayed on my
head while summoning
the Holy Spirit.

You showed me how. I
let my tongue slosh and
my vocal cords hum.

I must have done a
great job because both
of you smiled and gasped.

Then you let me go
back to watching The
Goonies in the den.

For the next ten years,
you'd drill me during
unbearable car rides,

"Are you using your
gift? Let's do some now."
I prayed we would crash.

I thought I was un-
godly but it was
fraud that made me squirm;

You buy it or not.
I was a liar.
Maybe so was God.

I guess you knew I
cheated. You never
trusted me at all,

never believed the
thing that was most true:
how deeply I wanted and needed you.

So I moved away,
quit my mother tongue,
had kids and designed

my own language to love them.

On Being a Mother and a Daughter on Mother's Day

My body knows - it never forgets -
that you stormed through it,
took what you needed,
left me with the remnants
of who I used to be.

You might, one day, say thank you.
You don't have to.
You might not.

I must replenish what I can,
as best I can,
in this new body
with this new mind.

You and others
- even some other mothers -
will want me always to put myself last.
Sometimes I should.
Sometimes I should not.
There's no guide for deciding
which and when.

Meanwhile, a version of me
inhabits your consciousness,
directing your thoughts,
teaching you to love
or loathe yourself.

If the latter, you will fight
to love me anyway,
feel guilty
for having to try.

There are no bad mothers.
This is not true.
But I need only be good enough
and raise a merciful judge in you.

We Saw Whales

(A reworking of Whale Day by Billy Collins)

Today I was awakened by strong coffee
and the notion that I might not see a whale
just like I didn't see the northern lights that night
we sat sipping cocoa in a frozen field in Iceland,
which was as disappointing as you might imagine.

As we ate our scrambled eggs, I didn't tell the children
that we might not find whales or that they might be introverted
and refuse our polite requests to see their dance.

Meanwhile, two Siberian humpbacks, wintering in Japan
were rehearsing their choreography,

crisscrossing one another, slaloming through
all those layers of green and blue in the East China Sea,
aware somehow of how the earth is busy with humans.

Can you imagine how it felt to see them fluke up dive,
peduncle slap and wave their pecs as if inviting us for tea,
or how the brave ones jumping in to swim with these supreme beings
could ever step onto a bus, consume a ham sandwich,
or stoop to pick up a coin from a pavement again
without the memory of that sensation
of being touched by and bound to the divine

under the sea? Will the children remember
this event as ordinary
the way they know most entertainment as dry fact
or will they store in their hearts the exhilaration
of the astonishing upheaval of water
and wonder how to tell their friends about the day they saw a whale.

Paradise is a Carpark Picnic

A stationary sedan full of restless kids
in a strip mall car park at dusk:
Dad is in the convenience store.
We've run our repertoire of games.

"Bored? On this island?
We're in paradise!" says Dani
from where she's sandwiched in the back seat
between my kids and hers.
"What's paradise?" they ask.
"The best place you can imagine," says Dani
who studies stars and black holes.
"It's not my paradise here,"
says my girl, "the sea was freezing.
And mummy wrecked my sandcastle."

It's true. The water was hostile.
She and I stayed dry
watching the others shiver
in the aquamarine.
I paced the beach
quenching fires on my phone
then strode right through the kingdom
she'd been waiting to show me.
The tide soon took the ruins anyway.

Dad comes back with a bag
of fried chicken and juice boxes for everyone.
On the radio, the Beach Boys
soften tired silence,
harmonising with contented sighs
and the smacking of slick lips
on greasy fingers.

Distance

On the call last night,
sipping wine in the dark,
I asked about work
and what it's like out there.

We touched on family things,
music tastes, penguins,
memories of school days
the humid weather lately,

and as I heard you fill the gaps
by filling up your whisky glass,
I wondered if the silences
were languorous or loaded,

if liquor was the only
tincture tingling your lips
or if words unspoken
lingered too, sip after sip.

Blood Moon

The children scramble up to the rooftop.
We used to come here all the time, before.
Was it ten years ago or ten minutes?

We witness the moon witnessing the earth,
bloodied by sunsets and concurrent dawns,
bright as a newly minted copper coin.

How long have we been standing here, waiting?
Ten minutes, ten hours, a thousand moons.
The kids are bored and cold. We go inside.

Food of Love

First, beer,
the white Belgian one you know I like,
offered in a frosted glass.

Fuck your beer.
My belly's still swollen with all those bloated things you said.

But it's not beer;
it's an olive branch, a token, an "I Remembered You."
It must not be refused.
The first sip sits fizzing in my throat
mingling with the bitter tannins of unspent ire.

Next, pasta.

Fuck your pasta.
The chilled summer dish I love with fresh tomatoes and basil
looks so refreshing on this sweltering day.
But fuck you,
I don't want it.

I do not want to want it.

"Chopsticks or fork?" you ask, setting it down.
"Fork," I say, with petty intent lost on you
or swept aside.

Then, pushing the first twist between gritted teeth,
I taste, clinging to loops of noodles,
a tang of I'm Sorry, a hint of Can We Start Again?
so sweet and smooth running through my lips
I can not get enough and suck them all up hungrily,
drink the soup straight from the bowl
and when I set my fork down
the beer is gone, the glass still cold.

I wipe my mouth with the back of my hand.
I understand.
I understand.

At the Kitchen Counter

It feels like a rebellion, sitting here with dishes in the sink,
emails to be read, children to pajama and corral into bed
but something keeps us at the counter slicing cheese with a butter knife,
drinking red wine from tumblers though there's crystal on the shelf
and then, like a loose tap, you start to drip
stories from your past,
details never shared in all these years,
cravings, insecurities, the heart's fissures
sealed now, now tough as the bread in our hands.

We tear strips from the staling loaf,
slathering them with liver spread, chutneys and
whatever else the cupboards yield,
wolfing them down between mouthfuls of wine and
laughter, so fresh it's like we don't know one another
yet; the notion of distance, a novelty,
moves us closer than we've been in years.
We clink cups and toast the people you have been,
the people you've been with and the man you've become
because of and in spite of me.

Loose Change

Our love has fallen
like loose change
down the back of the sofa
next to lint-clad half-sucked lollipops,
lego men and single socks,
waiting to be thrown out
with these forgotten things
when the springs are bust,
threadbare upholstery done to dust.

Or if it might be salvaged by a brave hand
groping blindly among mothballs
and bugs dining on biscuit crumbs,
would we want it still?
Desiccated and mildewed?
Could we polish it again
to look almost new?

Look at the Flower

Look at the flower:
petals, careful as a newborn's lids,
defend the filaments within
but watch how it sways in the feathery breeze,
submitting to rhythms no one can resist.

A draft chills your neck
but focus on the flower -
not the eerie ripple down your spine
like so many scuttling mites -

notice how tall it stands,
head bleeding a chaos of colour.
Don't strain to hear if the guns are drawing near
or run from room to room when earth convulses,
shifting plates pulsing underfoot,

come closer then,
focus on the microscopic motion,
see the flower breathe,
deeply in, slowly out.
Don't look away,

notice slender leaves lounging on their stem,
oblivious to the persistence
of the tight cold threat.

Zero in and listen
for a whisper:
“Keep your eyes on me,” it says,
“we’ll hold each other
while we can.”

Gress Beach

summer's faltering foothold has sunk into the dunes
tides flee into ashy clouds smothering the skyline

here is nothing
everything is here

baleful love
fraught peace
fertile void sturdy and dead as driftwood
and as beautiful

wind-flayed flesh splits
spitting up the blood of my forebears
it flows from me like the reticent tide
and seeps back into the machair
seabirds circle overhead
waiting to pick my ribs

this is how I leave the land of my ancestors
bent-backed peat cutters who lived
unspeakably rich
tough and spare lives

the salt air scours my core
scrubs my bones to pearl
this is how I leave:
father dead

my guts in the stomachs of gulls

What it Means to Miss You

It's not simply absence,
the *is not* of that which *was*,
like an empty slot on a shelf
where a novel used to rest,
or a pencil mark erased,
a you-shaped shape effaced,

your not being here
is a savage extraction,
the wound left in the earth
when a storm uproots a tree,
the volcanic rupture
of a tooth wrenched from its row,
Prometheus' liver
ripped out day after day.

So what do I do tomorrow
with everything displaced
by the cruel brutality
of your negative space?

Waiting at the Station

Another humid summer
six thousand miles from home.
Skin slick as vaseline
in the soupy midday slump,
I close my eyes and walk

with you, along our favourite path
through weeds and pampas grass,
the sun warming our backs
and, always, the loyal breeze.
We are holding hands,

greeting dog-walkers as they pass.
You know each name, each pain.
"Doctor," they say and tip their hats.
The bare-headed nodding instead.
We've walked this path

since I was small enough
for shoulder rides and piggybacks
and we both know this time
will be our last.
Carefully, as if our breath

might scatter them
like dandelion down,
we speak obliquely in half-whispers
of last things and last days,
our eyes fixed on the path.

A screaming train
yanks me back to the city stew
-no time to say goodbye -
so I leave you in the sunshine there,
the mellow breeze ruffling your hair.

Grief is a Needle

sailing through emails in the usual cafe,
on brew number two, not thinking of you,
when the fingerpicked Beatles riff
you used to play
slips into my ear

just like that,
the needle of grief,
stabs my marrow
swiftly as if
bones were butter

the quick prick clips my breath—

I pull it out,
that long and fine
spike,

tears of relief
hot as molten glass
soak the scarf held to my face

sobs subside
I settle down,
looking round
at all the people just
being

how much silent suffering
sits
in this room?

maybe we're all porous,
riddled with minuscule
puncture wounds

maybe this is how
love flows
in and out

Thoughts on Waking

Am I a poet?
I can not recall writing a single line.
But how could I?
There are no words in me.
Have I ever held a pen?

Who are these children in my house?
They plead for me ceaselessly
but what could I ever do for them?
Shards of memory cut my eyes.

My house? It's not mine.
Nothing is mine
save the dreams I dodge
in fitful sleeps.

In My Mind, I Don't Exist

In the vast abyss behind my eyes
I am a broad-brush daubing,
an impression, roughly human,
blurred oval with smudged features
grimly shifting in day-lit mirrors
to Mother, or others I've been,
never me, whoever that might be:
I cannot conjure a faithful shot.
Neither do I know myself

in either of my children.
But it's better this way,
saving me from vanity
(they are just so beautiful, you see).
But I was like my daughter
when I was her size
I know from all the photos
of a girl I do not recognise.
She always looks so happy.

Selkie

At ebb tide, in the depths of each night,
I pitched up on the rocks, shed my hide
and lay blissfully quivering in the haar,
admiring my moon-lit iridescent skin,
tracing maps of green and blue
to the throbbing hub where they convened,
stretching the sinewy lengths of my limbs,
touring undulations of stomach and hip
down to the soft brush, beneath silken furls
to my primary point of inquiry: a glistening pink pearl.

Life below the waves had become so lifeless.
Slipping through currents was a humdrum ballet.
I resolved to trick the magic beyond sundown
and thoroughly explore my human form:
to know it in repose and work and play,
feel sand sifting through fingers and toes,
to scale the hills that rose up beyond the shore,
beachgrass stabbing my fragile soles:
to master the shifting of muscle and bone.
But for all that, I'd need a chaperone.

One night, moon-bathing in the gloam,
I caught him watching, crouched in the dunes
and took my shot. Yes, it's I who went angling,
baited and stalked him, ruthlessly tangling
his heart in my nets. He froze as I sat astride
and rocked on him in the tall grass, singing my lullaby.
Half-drunk, he cried when it was done
then wrapped me in his coat, carried me home
and before I could think of my hide on the rock,
it had been stowed and the hiding place, locked.

It's interesting to hear what people will say
when they think you can't understand anyway.
Until I found my voice, they thought me mute.
My yelping attempts had them call me deaf too
though I ran when the babies cried or the kettle sang:
the primary requirements of a useful bride.
Over time, I learned how and when to speak,
and how to suppress my urges to scream,
but the words came out slowly, often in song.
They finished them for me and were always wrong.

My senses were keen. I was quick to adapt.
I learned to perform all my wifely tasks
while they appraised me like a beast in the zoo:
"Such taut, shiny skin and those eyes, Atlantic blue."
The women taught me how to sew and bake loaves
then sat at my table begging to know -
the oven, the grindstone, the sugar, the salt?
What set the flavour of my bread apart?
Even my husband could not understand,
the taste of the sea came from deep in my hands.

I gave that man three sons and three daughters.
He gave me warm furs but I longed for water.
The years closed the grip of the ring on my hand
and the skins of dead creatures pressed on my back.
Day by day, gravity burdened my bones
and I longed for the weightlessness of home.
I searched for my hide, dug holes in the ground,
pulled up the floorboards, hacked into the walls.
I wept by the shore where it had all begun,
gazing up at the hills where I'd never run.

Then, one afternoon I sliced my fingertip
and asked my girl for a rag to staunch it.
When she returned with a scrap of old leather
found in a hidden nook of a drawer,
I cast my skirt and blouse to the floor,
my wedding ring falling as if never worn,
and moments later, was bound for the shore.
I slipped into my hide and jumped in off the mound,
letting the sea reclaim me, further and further down,
further and futher until conscious thought seized,
further and further down, and was at ease.

I Am the Ghost

I am the ghost
not, as you suggested,
possessed by an evil presence;
there's no spook stuck to my back.
But how would you know that?

For years you've passed
right through me:
a phantom self
waning away the way
abandoned things fade.
You never hear me speak,
unaware I'm even here
until I sweep the table
wailing as the dishes crash.

I am the ghost
but I am coming back to life,
muscles rediscovering
how it feels to be touched,
fresh blood whips my veins,
colouring my lips again.
They part, poised
to speak new tongues.

Can you see me now
reestablishing my shape?
Do you hear my voice ring
in this emptying space?

My memory may haunt you
but my spirit will escape.

City Exhales

city exhales
last blazing breath
expelling hell from belly.
I, balcony-hidden from babies,
inhale forbidden cigarette,
each draw a sweeping audit
of a hard-stomached day.
above love hotel Caesar's,
smoke circle halo cloud
anoints each angel
aching under
holy neon skies.

A Garden and a Stick

My multitudes cannot agree
to party or pause
rage or recline
drink or detox
do work or do kids
stay up to read
or actually get some fucking sleep.

Why am I at war with myself?
Dear God, I'm never full,
never finished, never still—

oh! give me a garden and a stick.
I'll etch a poem in the dirt and learn it by heart,
the way we used to just remember things,

then I'll lie back on the lawn,
watching clouds race,
wondering how there could ever have been time for anything else
and the multitudes will
untie, unite
so softly
that the shush of grass growing,
will be muffled only by
the thundering shudder
of my heart throbbing in space.

Strike

then it swung out
splitting my skull
cleaving me clean
between night-blind eyes

the keen blade of clarity

I don’t want this anymore

Quiet Riot

Everyone is packing,
folding up folding chairs,
flinging unburnt kindling
back from where it came,
scouring tin cups
after tossing last night's beer,
scouring the grass
for fireworks and
fouled marshmallows.

I do not feel like helping.
I am rebelling.
Is that allowed?

I want to sit
here in this field,
the grass twitching with frogs,
wondering if we ought
to be cautious
with love.

Aren't hearts for breaking?
Is it foolish to want to feel good?

I feel them
watching me not helping,
eyes flitting to and from
my sun-warmed back
like butterflies.

Brittle grass jabs my thighs
but the frogs are singing.

Submit

I rearranged my dreams again
this morning, over tea,
in order of time sensitivity
and relevance in the Real World,
the one with deadlines,
bottom lines,
telephone and ledger lines.
Frown lines.
Waiting lines.

I have been waiting
for time and space,
inspiration, confidence,
for permission, for a sign
for every word to be perfect enough to
un-bench the fantasy that I might write.

I meant to.
Intent vaporized
to a hazy too-late-now,
wispy would-have-been-nice,
a shrug, a whim, a sigh.

But a sigh does not drip
like a broken tap
between your temples
as you wrestle sleep,
does not dog you
through years of neglect,
does not pine at the door
like a half-starved beast
aching to be fed.

I rearranged my dreams again
this evening, in bed,
in order of what brings joy to me
and to halt the nightly haunting
by these phantom aspirations:

I'll do what must be done
and willingly.

5 AM (part I)

I wake with the sun.
The dense serenity of resting souls
clasps me in this

sliver of limbo,
silver skies transmuting to bluest blue.
Water tastes so good.

On the balcony,
subtle breezes sweep my unadorned skin
like a bridal veil.

Brazen city rooks
leering jealously from utility lines
can watch all they want.

Hostile witnesses,
only birds, this morning, can verify
that I am alive.

5 AM (part II)

I exit the club,
smoke and sweat clinging to hair and bare skin
like rhythms to hips,

spellbound by spirits,
revived by strangers who remind me
I am still alive.

Hailing a taxi,
muscles exhale and dreams sweep my body
softly as silk veils.

In slivered limbo,
silver skies transmuting to bluest blue,
water tastes so good.

At home, I welcome
the dense serenity of resting souls
and sleep with the sun.

Tequila Sunrise

I'm propelled to the kitchen by a lingering tequila buzz.
The Sunday morning sun's already dancing on everyone
and coffee's been brewed, the crossword's waiting still half-done.
I reach for the pan to make French toast, so grateful to exist
alongside strawberries and syrup, word games and kisses.
The radio blasts songs from the past; my present listens,
the night coming alive again in my freshly unleashed limbs.
I sway over the stove, spin to the fridge for butter and milk,
flip the dishwasher up with my toes, shut the drawers with my hips.
While the kids make headdresses from beads and build lego boats,
I check my phone for the night's debrief and blurry too-dark photos
from the club where we unshelved ourselves for the first time in so long,
filling up the room with our newness, celebrating success,
pleasure the only agenda, knowing nothing can suppress
women with nothing to prove and no one we want to impress
anymore. I flip the sizzling bread, slice the fruit, put away
the milk, set places at the table, place flowers on the tray
and serve breakfast, full-hearted, in the glow of a new day.

Gone, Another Summer

Gone, another summer
and I am getting younger.
I, who skirted the water's edge
at the mouth of June,
peering in, hoping to catch
a glimpse of myself,
have shed my clothes and
jumped in off the rock
not knowing how shallow or deep
the unplumbed pool.

Newborn,
no sense of nakedness
or the inverse of innocence,
how things are supposed to be
or what constitutes certainty,
I count up bloody love-bite bruises,
vampiric transfusions by
insects the size of babies' hearts,
wondering how and when
my body returned to me
with such urgency
and whether it's ever been
this taut, this alert,
so ready to exploit those fruits
squandered on unschooled youth.

In the trees, cicadas shriek
their ecstatic last
while my cells multiply.
Unfurling my fists,
I submit to the currents in my veins
and soak in the close of summer
feeling young,
growing younger.

The Nature of Things

I'm not supposed to be here.
I should be sipping cool water in a clearing,
leaning my back into the rugged trunk
of an owlish tree, observing
fall's first blushes, reflecting
on my latest loop of the sun.

I'm not supposed to be here,
stripped and prostrate, oscillating
between chicken skin and cold sweats
in the time it takes to spread or shed the quilt.
The ambitious virus thumbing a ride
on a handshake or kiss, has lassoed me
in my city flat and camped out in my veins
while a typhoon pummels the window panes
competing to do the most harm.
I pop a sleeping pill and submit:
let them strut and brawl it out.

I'm not supposed to be here
unable to even crawl from the bed.
Writhing like a pupal grub,
skin rippling deliciously
in the velvety fugue.
Is this captivity?
How long can I stay?
Silence pervades the house,
still but for the storm.
I soak in its richness like
Cleopatra in a bath of honeyed milk,
drinking the peace in this place
I am not supposed to be.

Meditating at Nachi Falls

I see a horde of ghosts:
infinite spirits hurled from the
cliff in a ceaseless stream,
dashed on the slim stone shelf,
nanoscopic drops spraying
the sound boulders below.
Will they ever return to this precipice
to plummet again?

The bluff breathes with me,
stretching and shrinking.
Totems emerge from the ancient rock-
Goddesses with the heads of beasts -
hidden 'til I'm still.

The flow is slow enough to carry
the soft cycle of a breath;
strong enough to break my neck.

What is more sacred than this avalanche of water
reforming the crust of the Earth as we watch?

Nothing.
Everything.

The tear on my cheek.

The Shyness of Crowns

What is more sacred than trees?

Wiser than Solomon
older than Methuselah
stronger than Hyperion,
neither god nor mortal can compete.

Half-hidden palindromes,
their secret symmetry
conceals neuron-like networks
sharing nutriment, warning of disease –

Look up!

Crown shyness, they call it,
the way the tops stop just short of each other,
threading the forest canopy with sky-blue veins.
See how they stand so close as if agreed

to protect each others' solitude?
Not shyness then, at all, but the highest form of love:
leaving space to let the light in,
room to grow and breathe.

Spring Rain

The kids jumped puddles this morning
in the warm spring rain.
Did you see them sprint and splash,
could you hear them squeal and laugh
from a world away?

Now we're building Lego houses
sprawled out on the floor,
quiet, like we used to be,
listening to Debussy,
thankful for the rain.

Kintsugi

Even the best wine
will drip from a fissured cup
but salvaged, tended
and mended with gold it
will for a thousand years, hold.

March

Light slips in swiftly as
symbols from poets' lips.
At spring's first blush,
we're all poets
hoping to bloom again.

We worship the new,
revel in verses of rebirth,
milk nature for meaning,
fish for signs to make sense
of the cycles of our lives
but the promises you make
under the blossom canopy
have been heard a thousand times
by the ancient weeping tree.

Spring is not new;
the cycle of seasons is all there is,
a loyal constant we pummel for conceits
to understand the transience
of our credulous souls.
The brightening sky
as frost alights,
green shoots strutting forth,
the eager bud,
all are indivisible deities,
not symbols for our
epiphanies.

Abandon metaphor.
Put your face to the dirt,
know the sureness of soil,
true against your cheek.
Lie awhile and listen:
a season dawns each day.

And So

And so,
let the sharp-toothed truth
tear the flesh from your chest
and dress the wound with love
(the seed of all grief is love).
remember,
joy is not the absence of loss;
it's knowing that all will be lost
but not today

Acknowledgements

This book is offered with deep gratitude to the individuals who encouraged me to write it. Without you, Carmela, these poems might never have emerged from the drawer, and perhaps they wouldn't have even been penned. To Lindsay, Bianca, Eugene, Chloe, and Sue-Ann, your kinship, support, and meticulous proofreading have been invaluable. A special note of thanks to Melissa for gifting me the line, "The Ripe Fruit Must Be Eaten." Heartfelt appreciation goes to Peter for your unwavering generosity and enthusiasm. I reserve special thanks for Annie Kurkdjian, who graciously permitted me to feature her painting on the cover. It's an absolute honour – I live in awe of your art. To Eleanor Brown, this book exists because of "Maiden Speech." Your work opened me to the possibilities of experiencing and writing about life as a woman. You are a pivotal figure in the story of my life. Lastly, to W, your belief in me and this dream is what brought it to fruition. Thank you, with all my heart.

Author Biography

Rachel Ferguson is a Scottish poet whose work has been featured in publications such as Tokyo Poetry Journal and Slush. "Thoughts on Waking" is her debut collection. She lives in Tokyo, and in her spare time enjoys singing and walking in the woods with her children.

Printed in Great Britain
by Amazon

41349126R00057